'ine

JUNK-BOX
JEWELLERY

First published in Great Britain 2010

A&C Black Publishers
36 Soho Square
London W1D 3QY

www.acblack.com

ISBN: 978-1-4081-2227-3

Copyright © Sarah Drew 2010

A CIP catalogue record for this book is available from the British Library

Sarah Drew has asserted her rights under the Copyright, Design and Patents Act,1988, to be identified as the author of this work.

Page and cover design: Sara Oiestad

Photography:Tom Barker

Commissioning editor: Susan James

Editorial assistant: Ellen Parnavelas

This book is produced using paper that is made from wood grown in managed, sustainable forests. It is natural, renewable and recyclable. The logging and manufacturing processes conform to the environmental regulations of the country of origin.

Printed and bound in China

JUNK-BOX JEWELLERY

25 inspirational budget projects

Sarah Drew

To Joseph and Alfie for finding me so many cool things on the beach.

Sarah Drew

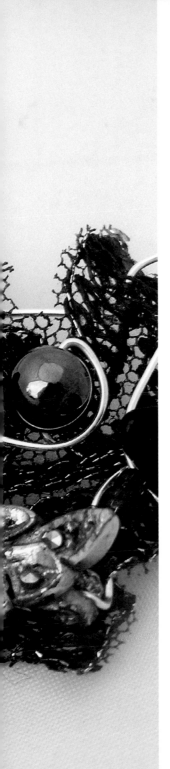

contents

introduction

Ever since I started making jewellery 20 years ago I've never had much money for materials. I began by spending some of my £4-a-week paper round money on beads from jumble sales and charity shops in York to make into those great, big beaded '80s earrings no one would be seen dead in now.

I used to take a jaunty little blue cassette case to school and flog them to teachers and friends like a little market trader. That progressed into making chunky fimo beads and acid-house flowers to impress my mates at uni; and onto Australia, using beach finds and pebbles to make jewellery that bought us a couple of dollars of petrol to get us a bit further round.

It didn't really matter, having no money. I never really expected to spend much on making jewellery. And after a while I actually started to appreciate the inventiveness needed to make things out of what I could find or get my hands on cheaply: the quirky, odd things I found, or already had, led the way really. The funny broken brooch, or the chunky 30s beads, or the rusted washers from my Dad's garage were all starting points for a design; and my lack of money really did make the creative part of my mind concentrate and come up with better ideas. I couldn't afford to buy exactly what I might have wanted to use (e.g. expensive stones, real silver and gold) so I looked at what I had, or could manage to get; and my design was taken down another avenue by a vintage button, for example, or a piece of weathered sea glass.

And what is also really lovely is that a new piece of jewellery you make in this way carries the previous associations of the objects you have used – the life the bit of plastic or vintage earring or antique button had before. You wonder who else wore that earring, which dress that button fell off; how far that piece of plastic has travelled, and for how long. And what's more, if you use things given to you by someone you know, you're really creating a new object that carries some personal history unique to that person, your friendship or your shared experience of a place (a pebble collected off the beach on a precious holiday, perhaps). So, without wanting to sound too touchy-feely, this new piece of jewellery you have made from given/found materials is carrying a measure of love or memory in it which can make you feel or remember whenever you wear it. I think jewellery with real meaning is very precious.

In this way, recycled jewellery is not a compromise at all. It may have started out that way for me – necessity being the mother of invention, and all that. But I now love using things that are old, that have had a life and a meaning, and look well-loved. They're a very tangible connection to the past (in the case of vintage brooches/buttons/beads/lace) or to a geographical place or geological process (in terms of the erosion of pebbles or the weathering of sea glass). They're a way of wearing history or geography which, if you're lucky, may be personal to you.

The frugality involved in not using loads of new materials, and not providing a market for new resources to be used up on your behalf, seems right at the moment too. It's nice to feel like you're making full use of what you already have at home, and probably a relief from the guilty feeling of thoughtless consumerism. And it's satisfying to use things that might otherwise have been chucked away; you can rescue them and make them into a new object that is beautiful and will bring pleasure. In light of what we surely know now about our overconsumption of resources and the effect that this will have on our planet, a slowdown and a return to thrifty values must make sense and could actually be a nice and quite relaxing way of life, taking away the pressure of greed and getting us back to the right way of doing things.

Making recycled jewellery is good if you have family too: it fits in well with looking after a barrage of unruly kids and animals. You can drag them out with you into the fresh air to burn off some of that limitless energy and employ them in collecting materials for you to use in your jewellery. My lads do actually love it. Granted, they might sometimes pick up massive, unusable pieces of unweathered plastic catering tub, or scary-looking shards of glass that have **not** been lovingly smoothed by lapping waves. But they do also find loads of smooth little bits of driftwood (and they don't mind foraging about in the stinky tideline seaweed for it) or lovely little gem pieces of sea glass that I might have missed. To be honest, it's less fun taking them foraging in junk or antiques shops, which can be a very stressful business. On one occasion, for example, my 3-year-old 'sorted' a basket of vintage lace doilies and had moved on to enthusiastically lifting and banging down lids on little antique mustard pots before I decided it was time to leave and come back later on my own.

I wanted the projects in this book to be as little fuss and bother as possible; so all the instructions I've included are aimed at complete beginners: no jewellery-making experience at all is required. If you have done a bit, I expect you won't read the instructions word for word (I never do), but I hope you'll be able to have a rummage through to get the gist and find plenty of ideas to help you make things according to your own meandering, creative path.

This book has been designed for you to be able to use the projects as a starting point and mix and match techniques as you go, adding your own skills and creating different looks depending on the materials used. Towards the end of the evening courses I teach in Cornwall in Southwest England, we have skill-swapping sessions. These are really effective – a fresh mix of other craft skills ranging from card-making to embroidery and even electronics, all shared so as to expand everyone's skill set. And it opens your mind to new materials and mediums that can be used, which might never have been intended for jewellery-making.

These projects are fine for beginners, and the techniques shown require very few specialist tools, which means you can make this recycled jewellery on your knee in front of the telly when the kids are in bed, or at the kitchen table, or even in the staffroom at work.

If you go to local markets and DIY shops you should be able to put together a basic toolkit for under a tenner, something that you'll be able to carry around with you wherever you go, so that you can create as the mood takes you.. I made the complete stock for a Cornish craft fair on a wet Welsh camping holiday last year: mud up to the top of my wellies, rain hammering on our 'sun' parasol, making crocheted sea-glass bracelets with my mum.

If you do really get into making recycled jewellery and you fancy having a go at selling some, either subsidising it as a hobby or as a tentative step into self-employment as a jewellery designer, I've put together a chapter with a bit of advice and some good sites to have a look at. I've found making jewellery a brilliant way to be able to look after my lads full time and earn money doing something creative that I really enjoy.

If you have small children and you are housebound in the evenings, it's no hassle to spend a few hours making pieces that you can sell at work, at a weekend craft fair or even on eBay. Kids or no kids, it's also a very low-risk way of trying out a new direction if your present situation looks a bit uncertain, or you've just had enough of a boring job. And if you can keep your costs down by using found and recycled materials it makes good business sense as well as beautiful design sense. Anyway, let's get cracking with making some jewellery.

getting
started

Basic tool kit

You should be able to get the basic things you need to get going for under a tenner, especially if you can get to a market with a decent tool stall and can order your findings and wire online. Then, if you get into making jewellery, you can spend a bit more as you go along, perhaps buying a multi-tool for drilling and polishing (£30) and maybe eventually tools and materials for making pieces with sterling silver (£50–£100). But that's further along the line. All you need to begin with are:

pliers: small, flat-nosed ones are best (it helps if they've got grooves to grip with)

snips: again, small so that you can get in to finish off your designs neatly

wire: silver-plated copper-core wire is popular and easy to use: if you can get some in 0.4, 0.6 and 0.8mm, you should have most styles covered

tigertail: you can buy it cheaply online (see websites at the back of this book) in 10 or 20m (33 or 66ft) lengths

findings: clasps, jump-rings, extender chain, crimps

crochet hook: different sizes produce different effects, so try and get a couple if you can

glue: superglue is useful (the liquid one) and maybe Araldite.

Ideas for recycled materials

Lots of small things can be used to make jewellery - the list is endless really, but the following work well: antique buttons, antique pearls, antique crystals, old chain, vintage earrings (1950s clip-ons), old diamante (to be cut up), small charms, broken jewellery, washers, nuts, rawlplugs, old keys, coins, old silk flowers, vintage lace, sea glass, sea plastic (weathered), sea string, driftwood (small bits!), pebbles, shells.

Where to find things

Beaches Not necessarily the prettiest, unfortunately. They clear away sea plastic/string and driftwood on pretty tourist and National Trust beaches, so sometimes you have to go early in the morning or else to slightly less picturesque locations in industrial areas.

Car-boot sales As any avid car-booter knows, you do often have to sort through a lot of useless stuff to find your treasure, but persevere as you'll probably get a good price, especially if you haggle a bit. Be a bit wary of dealers if you don't want to pay over the odds.

Jumble sales You don't see as many as you used to, as I think they've been a bit usurped by car-boots. But if you can get to one, you may find it a happy hunting ground if the church ladies happen to be throwing out their lovely 1930s brooches and beads.

Charity shops Old, unpolished, obscure shops often produce the best finds, I've come to realise. I think some of bigger organisations send their best gems off to auction houses. Of course I don't begrudge them getting the best price for their donated goods if it furthers the charity's cause, but it's a bit of a rubbish result for cheap-antique foragers like us. However, you can sometimes ask if they have broken bits they will spare you. Alternatively, do as my grandma did and get a part-time job in one so that you can pick off the best bits as they come in. Scandalous!

Little antique shops/stalls Some specialise in brooches, for instance, and these will have loads of choice and won't be too bad on price either. Again, you could ask for broken bits – it is easy to replace stones, especially clear diamante, with a blob of superglue.

eBay Good old eBay! Very convenient if you're after a specific colour or era or look, as you can put in a search for it and have potentially loads of choice. It's a good idea to set yourself a limit so that you don't get tempted to spend too much, and it helps if you get bit of experience of last-minute bidding so that you don't push the price up.

Relatives Make it known to all friends and family that you are now making jewellery and would appreciate any old bits of jewellery, buttons, even plumbing supplies they would like to donate. Accept with gratitude strange, perhaps unpleasant-looking items: they all add to your collection, and I bet you'll find a use for them eventually; if all else fails, make them into some earrings to give them for Christmas...

Your junk drawer Everyone has one. Good for quirky charms (e.g. a toy version of Thunderbird Scott's mini, plastic radio), odd sparkly earrings, threads of strange textures to crochet (e.g. an old mobile charger cable).

Your garage/DIY store Washers, nuts and strange things you don't know the use of (and will probably need next week and have to wrench off your bracelet) look cool as charms and nice as linkages in long necklaces. DIY stores are good for all types of glue, cheapish tools and silver or gold spray paint too.

Cheap local markets Good for even cheaper tools (£1 each for pliers and snips at my local market), silk flowers, haberdashery stalls and glues.

Sale bins Accessories stores sometimes offer ridiculous discounts on certain items or else 10 things for fiver. Get lots of chain and loose beads that you can cut up and get a load of mileage out of. Do not be tempted by the ear muffs.

Your own jewellery box Bet you've got lots of bits you really haven't worn for six years or more. If you can bring yourself to be ruthless, it might be an idea to make these into pieces you do actually want to wear.

Recycle centres Some areas have scrap shops with quirky bits of plastic and odd material offcuts available.

Furniture shops Places that sell leather sofas sometimes have swatches for sale or maybe even for free. You can get a selection of colours in good-quality thick leather.

Craft/bead shops Some have excellent supplies of jewellery-making things. Some don't, but you can still find other things you could mess about with to produce new and wonderful designs. In some shops, you can pay a bit over the odds for things like wire (though sometimes it is best to buy this online or by mail order); on the other hand, it is nice to see beads and compare colours, size, etc., before you actually buy, so shops you can actually visit have the edge in this regard.

Websites/mail order There are loads of bead websites around where you will probably get the best deal on wire and findings (catches and rings, etc.) as well as any cheap filler-in beads you might need. My own favourites are in the list of useful websites at the end of the book, but if you're after something specific a search in Google will probably bring up loads more. The first few of my own choices offer catalogues you can telephone for if you prefer.

vintage treasure

1950s-style linked bracelet or necklace

You will need:
- about 1m (3ft) of 0.8mm wire (silver-plated or gold-plated is good)
- flat-nosed or round-nosed pliers and snips
- a collection of antique beads
  - a small silver/gold hook

1. Cut a piece of wire around 5cm (2in.) long (longer if you're using very big beads).

2. Thread your first bead onto the wire and make a loop in one end by bending about 1.5cm (⅝in.) of the wire away from you at a 90-degree angle (see the picture) and then looping it back towards you using the pliers, so that the loop is centralised when you put the bead on.

3. Bend the loop round so it sits in the bead hole, then snip away any extra wire and neaten up the loop join.

This is a good, simple way to use up odd or broken vintage glass beads: you can incorporate all different shapes and sizes to make an elegant, retro bracelet with a lovely eclectic feel to it.

4. Make a loop at the other end in the same way as before, cutting off any extra wire.

5. Repeat the process above, then attach this bead to the first one by threading the wire through the loop (of the original bead) before you close it up.

6. Keep adding beads in this way to form a chain. Make it long enough to go round your wrist and then maybe add an extra bead for a dangle charm.

7. Attach a hook onto one end of the bracelet (see p.23 to learn how to make your own).

8. You can do it up by either hooking into a loop or next to a bead: you'll probably have a bit of flexibility regarding how loose to wear it, depending on how you feel.

Top tip: Use this technique to make short sections for a long eclectic necklace: you can combine them with pieces of suede, ribbon or beaded tigertail for a bit of a mixed-media look.

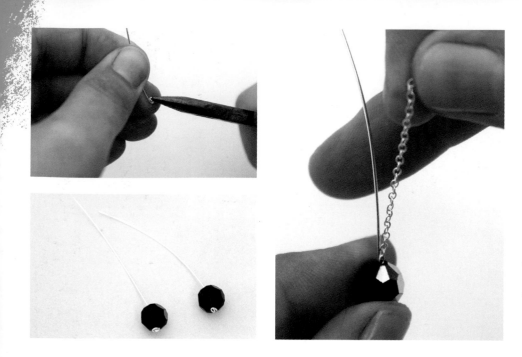

elegant deco style earrings

You will need:

- two gorgeous beads (vintage crystals/pearls or glass ones are nice)
- about 10cm (4in.) of fine chain (with large enough links to get wire through)
- 1m of 0.6mm wire (0.4mm if the bead holes are very small)
- (optional) earring wires if you don't want to make your own

1. Break up your vintage necklace with the snips so that you can extract the beads that you want to use.

2. Cut two pieces of wire about 6cm (2 in.) long. Make a snail ending at one end of the wire by making a small loop and turning it round against the wire one more time. Then bend it at a 90-degree angle so it makes a small ledge.

3. Thread your beads onto the wire.

4. Cut two pieces of chain about 2–3cm (¾–1¼in.) long (longer if you'd like exaggerated, focal earrings). Start to make a loop at the other side of each bead but don't close it up.

5. Thread the loop through the bottom link of each piece of chain.

6. Close up the loop and snip off any tail ends.

7. Cut a length of wire around 4–5cm (1½–2in.) long and start to make a very small loop on one end. Thread the other end of the chain (the one without the bead) onto this loop and close it up.

8. Using your thumb and fingers, gently ease the wire round into a smooth curve to form the earring wire. You can make a feature of the wires by making them a bit oversized, or for a

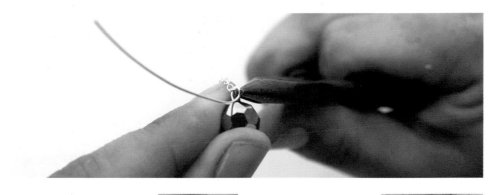

more traditional or antique look make them about 1cm (½in.) long.

9. Snip off any extra wire and carefully file the end of the wire so that it doesn't feel sharp. It's important to spend a bit of time getting that right as your

Top tip: if you fancy having a go at a more clustered style of earrings, you can use this same technique but just attach more pieces of chain with a bead 'dangle' onto the same earring wire: a bit more of an 80s rock chick look!

ears are very sensitive to little scratches from sharp metal.

10. However, don't go too mad as the copper might start showing through or you might bend the wires out of shape.

11. Make another ear wire in the same way as above: try and get the same shape and size as the first by holding them next to each other.

12. Check they hang right and are the same length by dangling them from a pencil or file.

13. You can buy earring wires if you want to save a bit of time, but I think they sometimes spoil earrings by not balancing the style out or looking a bit generic.

If you've got a couple of beads that you really love, this is a good way of making a real feature of them. You can also use up any bits of broken, antique chain you might have lying about. It's very straightforward and you end up with lovely, sophisticated earrings that are very flattering.

You can achieve quite different looks with this technique depending on which combination of beads you choose. For a satisfyingly sleek vintage look, use beads of the same size and colour, perhaps vintage crystals or pearls. Then you can attach an antique brooch for a focal point.

If you use an eclectic mix of vintage beads or stones in different colours, you get more of a soft hippy look, which is equally attractive. How you make your choice will depend on what you want to wear with the choker and also the type of beads you have in your box.

lovely retro plaited choker

You will need:
- Three lengths of 0.6mm wire about 50cm (20in.) long
- masking tape
- about 30–50 same- or similar-size beads
- some extender chain or ribbon (plus clamps)
- a lobster clasp
- pliers and snips

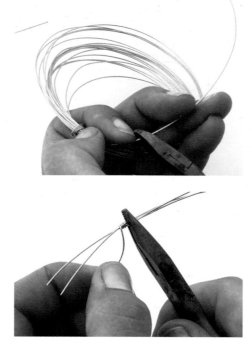

1. Using your snips cut three lengths of wire around 50cm (20in.) long for a bracelet and 70cm (27½ in.) long for a necklace.

2. Hold the pieces together then wrap one of the lengths around the other two about four times, leaving 3–4cm above the wrapping (see picture), so that you can make a loop at the end with which to attach the clasp.

3. Snip off the extra tail end and stick the wire lengths to a table or tray with masking tape. You're now ready to start plaiting.

4. Thread a bead onto the right-hand wire length.

5. Then cross that over the middle wire so that it becomes the new middle wire, in the same way that you would plait hair.

6. Thread a bead onto the left-hand wire and cross it over the middle one so that it becomes the new middle wire as before. The first few beads are a bit tricky to get into place: they should sort of sit diagonally next to each other.

7. When you cross the wire over the middle one, don't do it so tightly that it lodges under the bead and pushes it out of place.

8. Keep the tension quite firm and continue threading beads onto the side wires and plaiting down as above. It really is just like plaiting hair, while adding a bead to the side wires each time.

9. Stop 2–3cm (¾–1¼in.) before the bracelet (or necklace) is the right size for you. This gives you space to add a clasp or a loop for ribbons. Do a plait each side without a bead to finish it off.

10. Wrap first one wire round the other two, then one of the two remaining lengths of wire around the last one, leaving just one length of wire (see picture).

Top tip: This style works just as well as a bracelet - just make the plaited part shorter to fit around your wrist in an oval shape, and maybe choose a smaller brooch.

11. Find the middle point of your chain and snip it.

12. You might need to take a couple of centimetres off the length depending how low you'd like the necklace to hang.

13. Start to bend the remaining wire into a loop, thread it onto one end of the chain, and close up the loop by wrapping it round the chain on itself. Do the same loop at the other end and attach the other end of the chain.

14. You might want to change the clasp and add an extender chain to fasten it up at the back, and it does look good if

you make a little bead charm drop at the end of the extender chain.

15. If you want to fasten the necklace with ribbon, just make loops and thread the ribbon through and tie a neat knot. Et voilà! It's finished.

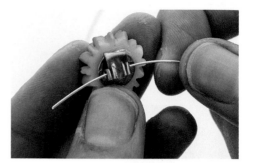

big bling dress ring

You will need:

- 100cm (3ft) 0.6mm wire
- about ten beads of various sizes
- a single focal bead (or an old earring or small brooch)
- pliers and snips
- a file

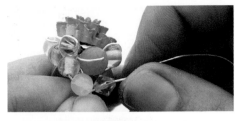

Top tip: You could make a big bling ring with a piece of Hepworth-wrapped sea glass as the focal point. Just thread it on as you would a feature bead.

This is a good way to make a feature of an odd button, 50s earring or antique bead you might have had lying about. You can combine it with an eclectic mix of other filler beads, maybe even a bit of lace, and you end up with a really striking, possibly sparkly, cocktail ring. They make really good presents and are great for bridesmaids and proms. A ring like this is a big, bold, dressy feature that will draw the eye away from your head and stop all the bling being top heavy.

1. Cut around 1m (3ft) of 0.6mm wire. Starting around 12cm (4¾in.) from one end, wrap the wire three times round the finger on which you'd like to wear the ring, though not too tight. Pull it off your finger, holding the loops together.

2. Wrap the short end tightly round the three loops three or four times to secure them, and snip off this tail end.

3. Choose one of your filler beads and thread onto a long piece of wire. Push it to the end towards the ring then loop the wire round the bead, from hole to hole.

   Wrap the wire once round the ring.

4. Thread on another bead and wrap it and tether it to the ring in the same way. Add a few more in this way, working in a vaguely circular shape.

   You might want to put your feature bead on after about four or five others, depending on their size.

5. Work around your main feature bead to frame it with the others.

   When you're happy with the number you have attached and with the ring's general shape, squeeze the design a bit tighter and then wrap the wire round the ring hand on the right.

6. Begin to tightly coil the wire around those three original loops. This task is a bit labour-intensive but still worth it for the resulting smoothness, which makes the ring comfortable to wear (as well as stronger, of course).

7. When you've gone all the way round the ring, wrap the wire round a few times under your design at the left-hand side, then snip it off and squeeze the tail end gently into place with your pliers. Try it on your finger – it might need shaping a bit. Otherwise, it's done.

There is a bit of a 1950s, lovely-and-ladylike, Grace Kelly feel to this necklace. It's quite a frugal piece, too, as you can get away with using an eclectic mix of leftover, similar-coloured beads for the beaded necklace bit. Lots of different styles of brooches work as the pendant drop: you just need to be able to get the tigertail through in a way that keeps the piece balanced.

grown-up antique tigertail necklace

You will need:
- a pretty, largish vintage brooch
- 40–50 mixed beads, depending on size
- 60cm (23½in.) of tigertail
  (or beadalon – 7-strand is best)
- about 10–20 crimps
- a lobster clasp and some extender chain

Top tip: You can get an even stronger-looking necklace by threading two or even three strands, with a large brooch as their focal point.

1. Get your brooch ready by removing the pin from the back. Using your snips, just snip through the pin first, close to the hinge and in a careful, controlled way.

2. Next gently snip the pin base in one direction then the other. The old base metals are normally quite soft and it may come away quite easily. If it's a bit tougher, just take your time and keep snipping round in different directions. Try not to pull the brooch backwards and forwards too much: you can end up snapping it or losing stones out of the front.

3. File any rough pieces of metal left from the pin, and now it's ready to be turned into your necklace.

4. Cut a piece of tigertail with your snips, about 30cm (12 in.) long. Thread two crimps onto the tigertail.

   Then thread the tigertail through the brooch on one side, pulling it through by about 5cm (2in.).

5. Thread the smaller 5cm (2in.) side through the crimps as well to make a loop. Push the crimps towards the brooch, quite close so that the loop is only a couple of millimetres long or as unobtrusive as possible.

6. Get your flat-nosed pliers and, firmly gripping both crimps, press down hard to squash them onto the tigertail.

7. Snip off the tail end piece: it should have made a good strong loop now, forming a strong base to thread your beads onto.

8. Then you simply have to thread your beads onto the tigertail. They look best random and carefully disordered, I think, and you can get away with a few quite chunky ones, depending on the size and style of your brooch.

9. When you've threaded on enough to make half the length of your necklace (I measure it by holding the brooch part where I want to sit and then seeing if the beads reach that round, knobbly bone at the base of my neck), thread on another couple of crimps and then thread the tiger tail through your extender chain and back down through the crimps as before. Squeeze firmly with your pliers, then that side is finished.

10. Thread the beads onto the other side in exactly the same way, put a clasp on the end instead of some extender chain. And then that's it, done! Instant 1950s glamour.

These chains are a great on-trend way of making a focal point out of something that makes you laugh! Kitsch things that you love even though you shouldn't can look witty and pretty on this feminine style of necklace. I made some with some tacky kitten and dog brooches I found, and they were really popular, probably with other people sharing guilty, tacky pleasures!

quirky-find chain necklace

- some lovely, little kitsch things, e.g. quirky earrings, a Sindy shoe, a little brooch or a plastic flower
- some old chain to cut up – quite fine, gold chain (gold-plated, probably) works well
- a lobster clasp
- some extender chain
- some gold-plated jump rings (maybe some big feature ones)
- pliers and snips

1. if you're starting off with a complete chain, find the middle point and snip the chain about 3cm (1¼in.) either side to open it up. Keep this piece of chain to reattach in the next step. If you're using old bits of chain, get two pieces ready, one about 2–3cm longer than the other.

2. Find another piece of chain about 2cm (¾in.) longer than this piece you've just cut off and get two large jump rings or feature rings sorted.

   Attach the jump ring to the end of the main necklace and also attach your two separate pieces to it.

Top tip: You could do a longer-style necklace along these lines with some large rings randomly placed and kitsch charms hanging all the way round.

3. Get another jump ring and attach the other end of the pieces of chain and the necklace end to it. You should have a kind of chain swag.

4. Cut some varying lengths of chain to add as drops that will hang from these jump rings: I think three on one and one or two on the other looks good in an unbalanced, asymmetric kind of way.

5. Now you can start adding your tacky charms. Get them ready by either attaching a jump ring, if possible, or by threading them onto some wire with a 'snail' loop at one end so that the charms don't fall off (see p. 18).

6. If you're using a small brooch, you might have to take the back off with your pliers and snips. Try to be careful not to bend it too much and wreck the front piece.

7. Lay out the necklace to see where you'd like to place things, then simply attach them either to the chain or the jump rings by opening up the charm jump ring (with your pliers), threading it onto the chain and closing it with your pliers. If it's a bead you're attaching, simply start making a loop, thread it though the chain, then close it up by wrapping it round on itself with your pliers.

8. Just check that your necklace hangs right by trying it on, and if it does then you've nearly finished. You might just want to put an extender chain and a new clasp on the back so that you can wear it at different lengths depending on what neckline you're wearing it with. And that's it: kitsch delight!

beach
found

This is a really useful technique to get your head round so that you can attach things you find which don't have any holes to all sorts of jewellery you're making, such as bracelets, pendants, earrings and even rings. It also looks quite stylish and simple and a bit 50s retro, so you don't have to resort to weird, frilly 1980s wirework styling.

sea glass hepworth wire-wrapping

You will need:
- a pebble or piece of sea glass you've found
- about 50cm (20in.) of 0.6mm wire (0.4mm if it's a small pebble)
- flat-nosed pliers and snips
- a chain or some suede or thread if you want to wear it straight away

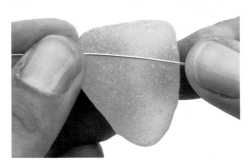

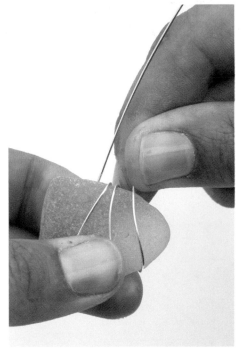

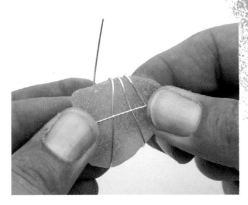

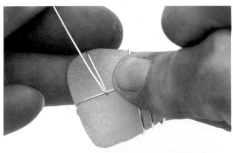

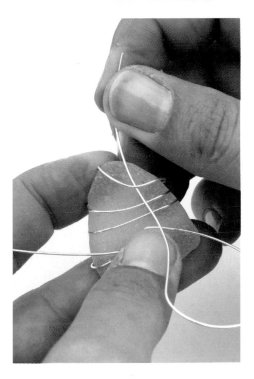

1. Using your snips cut a piece of wire about 50cm (20in.) long. Straighten it out a bit with your thumb and forefinger.

2. Holding the pebble or glass in your right hand, firmly bend the wire round the top corner, leaving about 5cm (2in.) at the back.

3. Take the wire across the pebble and firmly wrap it all the way around. Keep the tension as tight as you can and try not to let the wire slip.

4. Wrap the wire widthways three times around the pebble, then take it to the bottom and bring it vertically over the three wrapped lines.

5. You should have a sort of wire corner now that holds the pebble in place.

6. Take the wire over the top and twist it together with the 5cm (2in.) end you left at the back.

7. Thread the longer wire end through the bottom widthways wire wrap, and bring it back up to the top of the pendant.

   Wrap it around the twist to maintain the tension.

8. Snip off this end and make a loop by wrapping the other wire back around itself three times (I've done it here directly onto the chain).

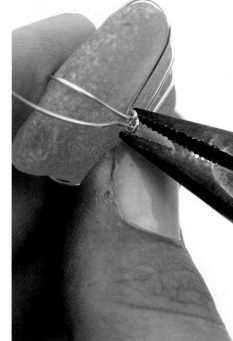

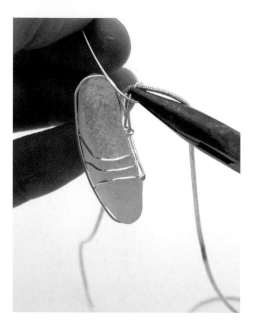

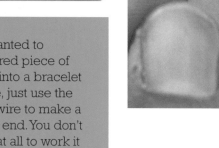

Snip off this tail end. Squeeze in any short bits with your pliers and gently file down any rough edges.

9. That's it, finished. You can wear it like this, as a pendant, or have it as a charm on a bracelet.

Top tip: if you wanted to incorporate a wired piece of glass or pebble into a bracelet or long necklace, just use the longer piece of wire to make a loop at the other end. You don't need any loops at all to work it into a bling ring or crocheted piece.

bit of everything charm bracelet

You will need:
- a piece of large linked chain for the base (enough to go round your wrist)
- smallish finds from the beach: shells with holes, sea plastic (drilled), sea glass (wrapped)
- bright glass beads or semi-precious stones (about 10 pretty ones)
- 1m (3ft) of 0.6mm wire
- 10 large jump rings
- a clasp or hook
- Two sets of flat-nosed pliers and one set of snips

This is a nice way to really showcase favourite or quirky finds from the beach. You can fill it up as much as you like, and it's actually enjoyable to build it up over time and add things from different locations that have different meanings for you (a bit like people used to in the past with traditional gold or silver charm bracelets). I've used a vintage bracelet I got for a fiver in my local antiques shop, but you could cut up an old chain necklace if you have one, or get a plain silver-plated one from one of the websites recommended at the end of the book (they're not very expensive). Happy beachcombing.

1. Lay your chain out on your work desk so that you can start to plan your bracelet. Decide where you want to place your main focal pieces first (e.g. the sea plastic) to give yourself a bit of design structure.

2. Attach the focal pieces to your chain first. Open up one of the large jump rings using the two sets of pliers and thread your piece of plastic (or shell) onto it. Thread the open ring through the place in the chain where you want it to sit. Then close it up again with both sets of pliers.

3. Get your other bead charms ready now: make a 'snail' ending (see p. 18) on a length of wire about 7–8 cm (about 3in.) long.

   Thread on your chosen bead and then prepare some more charms.

Lay out all your charms threaded onto wire so that you can plan their positions.

4. Bend the wire back at 90 degrees to start to make a loop. Thread the loose end of the wire through the chain then wrap it back round on itself a few times. Snip off the tail end.

5. If you have any odd things you'd like to thread onto the bracelet that can't be attached in either of the ways discussed, just get a piece of wire about 7cm (2¾in.) long and make a largish loop at one end. Then put the charm onto it, wrap the wire back around on itself a couple of times and snip off the tail end. Then take the

loose end of wire, and thread it through the chain and back around itself in the same way.

6. Attach the hook or clasp using a jump ring and check that it fits and looks OK by trying it on. You might see a few gaps when you do this and decide to add a few more charming charms.

7. Run your fingers over your bracelet to check that there are no sharp ends of wire left. If there are, squeeze them into place with your pliers and take a file or nail file and gently rub them down so they feel smooth to the touch. And that's it, done! A lovely, jangly, holiday-memory-laden bracelet.

Top tip: Make a sea-find necklace. You can either pile loads of quirky things on the front part of a chain, for a heavy, full look, or perhaps put some pretty, delicate finds on a finer chain for a light, feminine style.

beach find sea plastic necklace

You will need:
- Three to five pieces of weathered sea-plastic about 5–10cm (2–4in.) long (you could use sanded plastic pieces of lids or boxes if you can't get to the beach, and they could still be recycled)
- tigertail and crimps (about 20)
- sea string or lengths of suede/leather/ribbon
- a multi-tool drill or hand drill
- a chunky, eclectic mix of vintage beads and semi-precious stones
- Some cord, thin suede or thin ribbon

1. Get your plastic pieces ready by drilling a small hole in both ends of each piece using a small multi-tool (such as a Dremel). Make sure you rest on a surface you're not bothered about wrecking.

2. Cut a length of tigertail about 20cm (8in.) long. Thread two small crimps onto the tigertail.

   Then put it through one of the drilled holes in a piece of plastic.

3. Bend the tigertail back round to about 3cm (1¼in.) from the end, and thread it back through the two crimps.

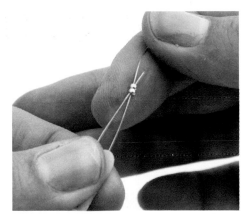

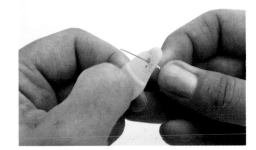

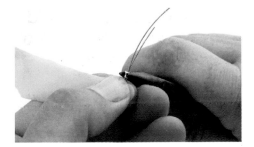

4. Using your flat-nosed pliers, squeeze the crimps very firmly so that they squash onto the tigertail and form a secure loop.

5. Put a selection of beads on the tigertail in a random manner, leaving yourself about 5cm (2in.) free at the other end so that you can attach another piece of sea plastic. You don't have to use up all of the 20cm (8in.) if it doesn't look right: just trust your eye to see what proportions work well with the size of plastic pieces you're using, and keep in mind how long you want the finished necklace to be.

6. Attach another piece of plastic using the crimps as before. Snip another piece of tigertail to attach through the other hole on this second piece of plastic and then thread more random beads onto it.

7. Carry on until you've connected all your plastic bits with beads. You could just attach the final piece of tigertail to the first plastic piece to complete the necklace or, if you'd like to make it a bit longer and have a comfy piece of leather or ribbon to go round the back of your neck, you can incorporate a length of leather or ribbon using clamps.

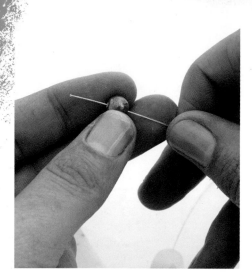

8. Make a loop on the final piece of plastic using crimps. Cut double the length of leather, string or ribbon that you need, and thread it through this loop.

9. Gather the two ends of leather or ribbon together and lay them in the clamp. Using your pliers, squeeze down one side to hold the leather in place and then the other side on top of the first clamp piece.

10. Then thread a small piece of tigertail (10cm/4in.) through the hole in the clamp and make a loop with two crimps. Put a couple of beads onto the tigertail then a couple of crimps.

11. Thread this through the clamp on the leather and squeeze to close up the loop as before. And there it is: big, bold and beautiful.

If you like big, bright, bold jewellery this necklace is perfect: you could wear a quarter of a weathered buoy around you neck as a massive statement necklace if you like. I've incorporated five smaller pieces of plastic on the necklace here. Teamed with chunky vintage beads and semi-precious beads the look is really modern and summery. Of course it does all depend on what you actually find on the beach, and designing your piece of jewellery around your favourite bits. It's good to think you're getting a cool, unique necklace out of clearing 'rubbish' off the beach too.

Top tip: You could attach some charms later on (as in the bit-of-everything charm bracelet).

Some little shells might look pretty dangling from the plastic or between the big beads.

fishing net cuff

You will need:
- longish lengths of sea string if you can find it
  (or another type of string if you're not near a beach)
- a nice mixture of sea finds such as shells with holes in,
  sea-plastic pieces and sea glass (small bits)
- big bright round beads (about five or six) – freshwater
  pearls and mother-of-pearl work well too
- 0.4mm wire (about 2m/6ft)
- pliers and snips
- a crochet hook
- a hook to fasten the cuff

1. Get a long piece of the sea string (or twine) and make a loop in one end by tying a knot.

2. Put your crochet hook through this loop (from front to back) and wrap the string once around the hook in a clockwise direction.

   Using the hook, pull the string through the loop whilst pushing the loop off the hook. You should have two loops joined now.

3. Continue with this movement so that your work starts to look like a chain. If you're not used to crocheting it's a bit tricky at first, so try not to get too cross

with it. Keep it loose with biggish loops – it really doesn't matter if it's a bit messy. You're after a higgledy-piggledy random look.

4. Make the chain just long enough to fit around your wrist, then pull the string through to stop the whole thing unravelling.

5. Now you're ready to attach some interesting bits and bobs. Cut a 1m (3ft) length of the wire and wrap it tightly around one end of your string chain four times.

6. Thread your beads and sea finds onto the other end of the wire – you'll probably need

between 20 and 30 depending on how full you want it to look.

Make a little loop at the end to stop them falling off.

7. Shuffle all these beads and finds to the end that's attached to the sea string. Put your hook through the first string-chain 'link' from front to back. Wrap the wire clockwise around the crochet hook and pull it through, pushing the string link off. The wire should now have a loop attached to the string chain.

8. With this wire loop on the hook, put the hook through the next string link. Push the first bead or

You can make this just with materials found at the beach (but you have to remember to take your pliers, snips and crochet hook with you): sea string from fisherman's nets, shells (with holes in them), pebbles and bits of sea glass. I have cheated a bit here and included some lovely bright beads, to signify buoys, and drilled my sea plastic because I'm lazy like that. But it's nice to know that if you felt like it on some fantasy Robinson Crusoe holiday, you could create something gorgeous just out of things you find.

find right up to the hook, then wrap the wire clockwise around the hook. Pull that wire through first the wire loop on the hook, then the string one. You should have one loop left on the hook – if you have, well done!

9. Keep going with this technique all the way along the string chain. You can be as haphazard as you like – just try and get some beads and finds to sit on the cuff in a cool, random way; it's supposed to look messy and sea-weathered.

10. To make a deep cuff, you might want to join on another 1m (3ft) length of wire and go back along the cuff, attaching beads

and shells, etc. in the same way as before. You can crochet this second (or third, counting the string) row onto either the wire chain links or the bottom side of the string links, depending on how you'd like it to look (more silvery and neat onto the wire links; more chunky and erratic-looking onto the string links).

11. When you've had your fill of crocheting, you just need to pull the end of the wire through the last chain link to tie it off. Then press it and shape it with your fingers until it sits in a nice circle or oval shape.

12. Next make a largish hook with a 4cm (1½in.) length of 0.8mm wire threaded through one end and wrapped back around on itself. Make the hook shape with your fingers and a little turned-up loop at one end.

13. You might need to trim the sea string with some small scissors to neaten up the ends a bit.

14. If you've sized it OK, you should be able to hook it in several places so that you can wear it looser like a bangle or tighter like a cuff, depending on how the mood takes you.

Top tip: You could make a similar-sized piece in exactly the same way for a bib necklace. Just bend the crochet work into a crescent-moon shape and attach chain or suede to each end so that you can wear it around your neck.

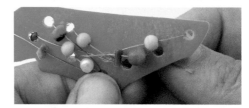

Sixties pin-art sea-plastic necklace

You will need:

- a largish piece of sea plastic (or sanded recycled plastic)
- 100cm (39in.) tigertail
- about 20 crimps
- a few small bright beads/stones
- a multi-tool drill or hand drill
- safety goggles
- pliers and snips
- fine sandpaper or nail-file
- a chain, torque or suede to wear it on

1. You need to start by drilling the holes into your piece of plastic, which is normally quite easy to do. Before you start, make sure you do it on a surface you're not bothered about, and be sure to wear safety goggles. Drill holes randomly, with some clustered together and some space left with no holes in. When you've drilled the holes, just sand down the surface a bit so it doesn't feel rough.

2. Cut a piece of tigertail about 40cm (16in.) long, thread a crimp onto one end and squeeze it into place about 0.5mm from the end.

Top tip: If you make up some of these pieces, you can incorporate them into other projects such as the crocheted cuff, the big bling ring or the sea-plastic necklace.

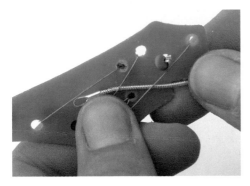

This a messy, colourful version of those funky, 60s pin-art pictures you see nowadays at car-boot sales and posh retro shops - the ones that create owls and butterflies, etc. from very neat lengths of thread stretched around pins. It's the same idea here, but the points for the thread (tigertail) are a bit more random, and I've included small beads on the wire to give a bit of extra interest and colour. You could keep the design a bit more minimalist if you like, leaving the beads off for an arty, Hepworth look. The choice is yours.

3. Thread a bead onto the tigertail, then thread the long end of tigertail through the plastic from back to front so that the crimp and bead stop the tigertail from pulling through.

   Thread a small bead onto this piece of tigertail, (at the front of the plastic) then pulling it very taut, thread it through a diagonally positioned hole (see picture). Take it back up around the back and pull it through another hole to the front, keeping the tension taut all the time.

4. Thread a bead onto the tigertail again and then thread it into another hole – you can use the same holes if you like. It looks good if the wires cross each other. Keep threading through the holes and around the back until all the holes have been threaded through.

5. Take the tigertail through to the back, thread on a crimp and push it right down to the plastic. Squeeze it and snip off the tail end.

6. You should be able to just feed a chain through the tigertail 'lines' at the back, so you can wear it as a cool, contemporary pendant. If you have a bit of trouble doing that, just thread a large jump ring through one of the holes near the edge and put it on your chain (or torque or suede) like that. If the ends of tigertail irritate your skin, you can just bend the bit with a crimp on, flatten it to the plastic and gently file any rough edges on the crimp or tigertail. That should make it more comfortable to wear.

use
what
you
have

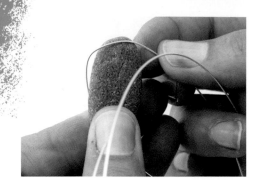

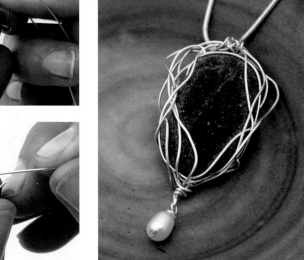

dreamy nouveau freestyle pendant

You will need:

- any old pebble, though one with a flattish shape and not too huge is best
- 100cm (39in.) 0.6mm wire
- a chain, ribbon or suede length to wear it on
- a clasp or some extender chain
- a little stone, pearl or bead for the drop

1. This piece is a bit freestyle. You just have to get hold of your pebble and start wrapping a length of about 50cm (20in.) of 0.6mm wire around it. Start from the top and wrap until you have a length of wire about 7cm (2¾in.) long sticking upwards (this will form the loop to attach the pendant to a chain later). Then bend the wire around the top corner and then around the back of the pebble.

2. Bring the wire back round to the front left-hand side, then take it to the back again and wrap it once around the wire at the top. Keep holding the pebble firmly, as it's not yet secured.

3. Take the wire in the opposite direction now. So first of all at the front on the top left and around the back; then at the front at the bottom right and around the back; then wrap it around the top piece of wire again.

4. Now you should have made a loose, wavy, nouveau cage for your pebble.

5. Once it is secure, think about how you want it to look. Perhaps bring the design out a bit at the top two corners, pulling it into a 'V' at the bottom. If you smooth the wire with your thumb you should be able to work some lovely, fluid lines around the pebble.

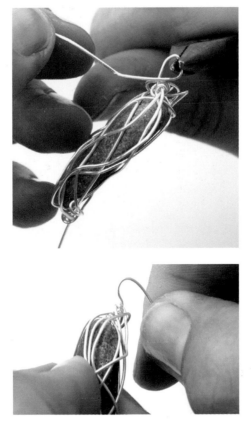

Top tip: For a more ornate necklace, you could make two separate nouveau wirework pieces (about 4cm/1½in. long, in a similar wavy style) to link with chain either side of your pebble drop.

You can tether the wire down a bit by wrapping it round at the top or the bottom of the pebble.

6. When you're happy with how the wire frame looks, finish off by wrapping the wire round it two or three times, making a smallish loop and snipping off the tail end.

7. Get your pendant drop ready by making a little 'snail' ending on a 6cm (2 in.) length of wire. Thread your bead on, bend the wire in a 90-degree angle

and start to curve it into a loop. Thread the wire through the pebble framework at the bottom of the pebble V before closing the loop by wrapping the wire back around itself at least twice.

8. The pendant should be able to move so that it dangles nicely. Make a loop, with the wire left at the top of the pebble, and snip off the tail end. File off any rough edges gently and it's ready for you to put on a chain or ribbon and wear with a dreamy, slinky, bias-cut dress.

This is a lovely way of making a very normal pebble, of the kind you could find anywhere, into an alluring, whimsical, art nouveau-style necklace. A flattish, slightly irregular shape is easiest to work with, and you can pick out a favourite stone to dangle from the bottom as a pendant drop.

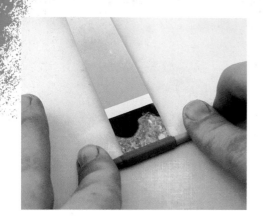

Top tip: The colour of the magazine pictures you use does make a difference if you want to keep control over the colour scheme of your necklace.

1. Cut some long strips of magazine – they should be slightly tapered at one end, like long triangles. Each strip will become a bead.

2. Wrap the fat end tightly around your pencil and then spread PVA glue thinly starting from the fatter end of the strip. Carefully and tightly roll the strip around the pencil so the glue is keeping the roll tightly wound up.

3. You might need to put a bit more glue on the end to seal the bead. Take the roll off the pencil and thread it onto some twine. Paint the bead with some clear varnish to seal it and then hang it up to dry.

4. Make as many beads as you need in this way and leave them to dry overnight.

5. Choose some other beads that co-ordinate well with your paper beads: chunky stones, vintage plastic or wooden beads would look good.

6. Cut a long piece of cord or suede and start threading the paper and the coordinating beads onto the cord. You can either leave them free to move about or make knots to separate them.

7. When you've got enough beads on your cord, make sure it fits over your head and then tie a knot at the back.

bright and shiny paper-bead necklace

You will need:
- old magazine pages
- PVA glue
- clear varnish
- a thin round sticklike object, such as a pencil, dowel or screwdriver
- some cord, thin suede or thin ribbon

They used to make beads like these in the 1930s, so with this project you're making something out of almost completely recycled materials and, what's more, a lovely vintage look. For an eccentric, Bloomsbury-looking necklace you could mix these beads with odd, chunky beads you might have lying about.

toolbox bracelet

You will need:

- some chain with big links: I used an old recycled plug chain but you could also use a silver charm bracelet or old watch chain. You can buy silver-plated chain quite cheap, or buy an antique chain at eBay or Carboot (see websites list at the back of the book).
- 0.6mm and 0.8mm wire
- spoils gleaned from your toolbox such as old washers, bolts, unidentifiable plastic things and rawlplugs, whatever you like the look of
- pliers and snips (two sets of flat-nosed pliers is useful)
- 10 chunky jump rings (5 or 6mm/about ¼in.)
- some round beads (haematite looks good)

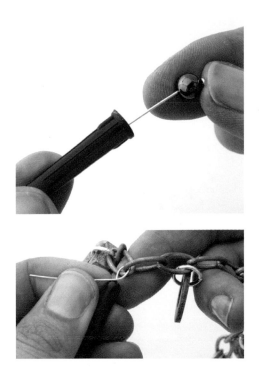

This bracelet is a multi-sensory delight: not only does it look really cool, it makes a very satisfying tinkly clanging noise whenever you move your hand. It also smells quite nice – that is, assuming you find the macho smell of oil and metal and rust enticing.

1. Lay out your chain on your work desk so that you can start to plan your bracelet. Place the toolbox charms vaguely where you want them to go so that you've got a loose design.

2. Prepare the components, such as washers and nuts, that can be attached with jump rings. They look quite cool a bit worn and rusted, so don't worry about cleaning them up.

3. Open up one of the jump rings using the two sets of pliers, and thread your washer or nut onto it. Thread the open ring through the place in the chain where you want it to sit. Then close it again with both sets of pliers.

4. Put the other washers and nuts on, spreading them out along the chain in the same way.

5. Get your other toolbox charms ready now, beginning with the hole plugs. Make a 'snail' ending (see p. 18) on a length of wire about 7–8cm (about 3in.) long.

   Then thread on a 6mm (¼in.) round bead (such as haematite).

6. Using a needle or pin make a small hole in the top of the hole plug, then put the wire with the bead through this hole so that the bead sits at the bottom of the hole plug.

Top tip: If you are feeling ambitious you could do a whole toolbox chain belt, for a subversive Chanel look. You can buy 'plug' chain from DIY shops – if you get some and load it up with charms in exactly the same way you'd get a cool, jangling belt that could even double up as a long neclace.

You might need to use 1mm wire for a belt – it's a bit tougher.

7. Get a few of these charms ready in this way, then thread the loose end of the wire through the chain and wrap it back around on itself a few times. Snip off the tail end.

8. If you have any odd plastic things you'd like to thread onto the bracelet, get a piece of wire about 7cm (2¾in.) long, make a largish loop at one end and put the charm onto it, then wrap the wire back around on itself a couple of times and snip off the tail end.

Next take the loose end of wire, thread it through the chain and back around on itself in the same way.

9. Make a loop in a length of 0.8mm wire and attach this to the end of the chain for the hook. Make a hook shape with the wire and finish with a tiny loop so that it doesn't feel sharp. Run your fingers over your bracelet to check that there are no sharp ends of wire left. If there are, squeeze them into place with your pliers, take a file or nail file and gently rub them down so that they feel smooth to the touch.

10. And that's it. The great thing about charm bracelets is that they look excellent when they're overloaded with stuff, so you can just keep adding random charms to it whenever the mood takes you. If you get a bit bored doing DIY one rainy Sunday, just nick a few bits and bobs and add them to your clunky, chunky bracelet. Big bright beads and even small lengths of electrical cable might look good too. Use whatever you can find.

midsummer
night's dream
twig tiara

You will need:
- some found twigs (green and not too thick)
- 2m (6ft) of 0.4mm and 0.6mm wire
- some freshwater pearls and rock crystal
- pliers and snips
- a small file

It might seem a bit odd wearing twigs in your hair for your wedding or ball or prom, but this design is surprisingly pretty and flattering. It's got that natural, slightly scruffy woodland-imp look that would work wonderfully for a woodland or Shakespeare-themed wedding. And it does look surprisingly good with other soft feminine dress styles to take the formality out of a look. You could make a more exaggerated version for a true midsummer night's dream: just add more twig rows, embellish it as much (or as little) as you like, and maybe build it up in the centre. It's a pretty, dreamy look that adds a quirky, ecological dimension to any occasion. It's also cheap.

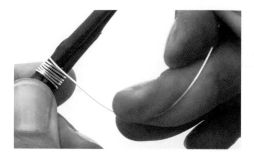

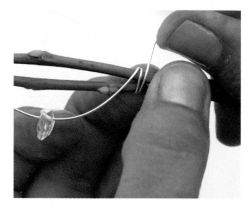

Top tip: For a bit more of a girly look, you could make little daisies with the pearls and wrap them randomly around the twigs.

1. Cut several twigs from the garden or woods: they need to be quite long, about 50–60cm (20–24in.), and bendy (so still green). Gently pull off all the leaves so that the twigs are bare.

2. Choose two or three twigs and gently ease them round into a horseshoe shape.

3. Bind one end with wire, wrapped around five or six times, then make a small loop so that you can grip the tiara into your hair.

4. Weave the sticks in and out of each other and, holding them firmly at the other end, bind

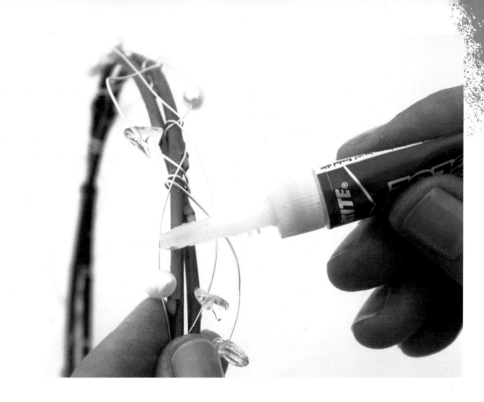

them together again with a 50cm (20in.) length of 0.6mm wire.

5. Bend the wire into a small hill shape, thread on a pearl and wrap it once round a twig or a bunch of twigs.

6. Now take the wire below the twigs, smooth it into a curve again, thread on a rock crystal piece and again wrap it around the twigs. Carry on like this until you reach the other end.

7. Wrap this wire around the end and join on another long piece, perhaps using 0.4mm wire this time so you can thread the pearls on more easily. Go back

the other way, threading on beads. Try and tether the wire in between the other hill shapes so it cuts into them. This gives a more art-nouveau look.

8. Make a few 'pointy' shapes from time to time, to break up the curves.

9. When you get to the other end, loosely wrap the two ends of the horseshoe together so that the twigs dry into the right shape. Leave overnight at least, then gently try on the tiara, grip-ring it into place through the little loops at each end.

Snip off the ends of the twigs,

10. If need be, consider sticking the beads in place on the wire with a small blob of superglue. And there you are, a lovely modern woodland nymph.

textile techniques

suede statement cuff

You will need:

- a piece of leather or suede that fits around your wrist (it can be any shape)
- a big press stud
- 100cm (39in.) of embroidery thread
- a stone or bead
- a large, sharp needle

For proper, efficient recycling this project is hard to beat: for example, I made about 30 of these once from an old leather skirt someone gave me. All different sorts of recycled leather, suede and fake leather could be used. You could transform a pair of dodgy leather trousers and get loads of cuffs from them (Christmas presents sorted). Offcuts from shoe companies or some of those rectangle leather samples from furniture shops would be good, too. You don't really need big pieces for cuffs, and sometimes the random, cut-out edges give you unpredictable, stylish 80s shapes with a more edgy design.

Top tip: if you get the hang of this project, you could do a double design of the graph with one half mirroring the other – it makes a square with an oval inside; or maybe loads of them randomly placed all over a cuff would look good.

1. Trim the leather with big sharp scissors (or a Stanley knife) so you're happy with the shape of your cuff.

   The ends should overlap at the back so you can get the press stud on easily.

2. Fold your suede in half and try it on your wrist. Mark a starting point for your pin-art design about 1cm (½in.) from the centre.

3. Cut a piece of embroidery thread about 40cm (16in.) long and separate the threads so that you have two lots of three strands.

4. Tie a double knot near the end of one set of three strands and thread the other end through your needle.

5. Starting at the top at the point you marked, bring the needle through from back to front. Take

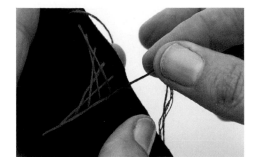

the thread in a vertical line for about 5 or 6cm (2–2½in.) and then take the needle through to the back.

6. At the back take the thread along about 0.5cm (¼in.) horizontally and take your needle from back to front. Once the thread and needle are at the front again, take it diagonally towards the top and enter the suede 0.5cm (¼in.) vertically below the initial top point.

7. Take the thread through to the back, and bring it back through at a point 0.5cm (¼in.) vertically below the last point. Take the thread diagonally downwards

and go through the suede at a point 0.5cm (¼in.) horizontally along from the last point. Have a look at the picture – you have to be quite accurate to get the neat, graphic effect from the thread.

8. Keep going in this way until your vertical point reaches the horizontal line. You should have a nice 'lined' curve on a graph axis.

9. If you have some left, take the thread through to the back and choose where you'd like your stone to sit. Bring the thread through to the front and thread on your bead.

Secure it with a couple of stitches from front to back and then tie it off at the back

10. Stitch the press stud firmly onto the two ends at the back: the 'female' part needs to go on the 'right' side of your cuff, the 'male' part on the 'wrong' side, so that they sit on top of each other when you bring the two ends around your wrist.

11. Check that it fastens and sits OK, and then it's done.

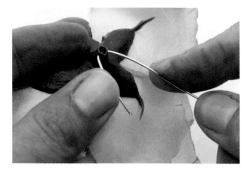

Billie Holiday flower headdress

You will need:

- some old artificial flowers
- a tiara base
- 1m of each: 0.6mm and 0.4mm wire
- some sparkly crystals (about 20) and sequins
- pliers and snips
- small file

1. Pull a bunch of the artificial hydrangea flowers off the main head and wrap them tightly with the 0.6mm wire, leaving a longish tail to attach the flower to the tiara base.

2. With a needle, make a small hole in the plastic back of the rose. Then you can get some wire through (a 15cm/6in. length of 0.6mm wire should be fine) to wrap into a tight loop so the rose is secure.

3. Think about how you want these bigger flowers to sit, then tightly wind them onto the side of the tiara base (it's best to stretch it into a horseshoe shape, as the circle shape is very uncomfortable to wear).

Top tip: If you'd like an even more decadent-looking headdress, get some old diamante to drape and dangle in lengths from the side, and maybe an old 30s diamante brooch to snuggle into the flowers.

This headdress is a real nod to the jazz era. It would look so cool with a slinky, bias-cut tea dress and some red shiny shoes – great for a boozy, afternoon tea party.

If you could get hold of some milliner's net, you could add a bit to sit over one eye for more of a 'daytime hat' look. Get this made and all you need are some crackly old records to get you in the mood.

4. Get the other, smaller flowers ready to wire onto the base by pulling out their old plastic centres (carefully so as not to break the hole) and replacing them with wired crystals.

   Cut a 15cm (6in.) piece of 0.4mm wire and fold it gently in half. Push a crystal to the top point and simply twist the wire to hold it in place.

5. You could add another crystal or sequin by threading it onto one of the ends of wire, folding it about 1–2cm (¼–¾in.) away from the first and then twisting the wire until it meets the first. You could put a crystal on the other branch if you like.

Then twist the two ends together, ready to wrap around the base.

6. Push the wire end gently through the flower centre so that the crystals sit at the front. It's now ready to be attached to the tiara base.

7. Once you've got all the little flowers ready, just play about with where they look good in the headdress design.

8. Finally, wrap them around the base as firmly as possible, making sure to squeeze in any loose ends of wire and file off any sharp bits.

   Then you're ready to slink off and find a crooner.

higgledy piggledy twisted necklace

You will need:
- about 100cm (39in.) 0.6mm wire
- around 20 leftover beads that look good together
- chain or suede
- clasp and extender chain
- a few jump rings

If you've got lots of odd beads and stones left over you can make a quirky, bold new piece with this technique. You could also work in old buttons, little flowers and sequins, if you've got them. Most things can be incorporated, depending on the colour or the look you're after. And once you've twisted the wire it becomes pliable, so you can be as higgledy-piggledy as you like and change you mind for the next time you wear it.

1. Cut a piece of wire about 50cm (20in.) long and find the middle point by gently folding it over.

2. Cross these two ends over and twist the wires together for about 1cm (⅜in.), leaving a loop at the top.

3. Choose the first bead (or button or sequin) you'd like to include, and thread it onto one of the ends. At the point where you'd like the bead to 'stick out', fold the wire, with the bead at the top of the fold, and start twisting the wires together as before but with the bead trapped in place.

4. Twist until you meet the middle point, where the two lengths of wire meet, then twist both wires together for about 0.5cm (¼in.).

   Next put a bead on the other wire end and twist it in place like you've just done with the first one.

5. Twist to the middle again, then, when you reach the point where the ends of wire meet, twist the two long pieces together for about 1cm (⅜in.). It sounds a bit complicated, but really it is quite easy and makes sense when you actually have a go yourself. And again, it doesn't matter if it's not extremely neat or looks a bit different to mine. This is just a way of suspending eclectic mixed beads to showcase them in a quirky-looking way.

6. If you're feeling adventurous, you could attach two beads onto the next branch. Trap the initial one as above, then don't twist all the way to the middle; do a couple of twists then thread on another bead.

   Then twist the wires together and finally twist to the wire meeting point.

7. Do the same on the other side branch, then twist the long wires together to travel along the main branch a bit. Remember to travel along the main branch like this periodically; otherwise

Top tip: Try twisting shorter branches and more beads closer together for a more clustered, Italian look.

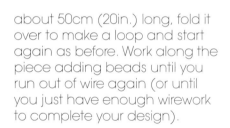

you end up with a radial, sunshine design (which is very nice as a pendant but not very useful here).

8. When your wire starts to run out you should have a piece of worked design about 8–9cm (3–3½in.) long. If you like the look of that, you can just make a loop with the wire and attach a chain with the jump rings. If you'd like the focal design to be a bit bigger (like mine here), you can make another piece in the same way and join them together in the middle.

9. Put the finished piece to one side but don't cut off the ends yet. Snip another piece of wire

about 50cm (20in.) long, fold it over to make a loop and start again as before. Work along the piece adding beads until you run out of wire again (or until you just have enough wirework to complete your design).

10. Next attach the two pieces together by simply wrapping the ends around each other onto the main branch. Snip off the tail ends and squash the wire into place with your pliers. You'll probably need to file it at the end.

11. Snip a chain in half and take some of the length off (try it round your neck and see how low you'd like the necklace to

hang). Then attach your twisty piece to the chain at both ends with the jump rings.

12. Attach a good clasp and extender chain at the back: you could make a little bead charm to drop off the chain at the back to finish it. This is a really useful technique to get the hang of (especially for bridal or special-occasion jewellery), and it can look really different if you use finer, 0.4mm wire and more delicate beads.

pretty lace choker

You will need:
- some vintage lace (an open design with embroidery or beadwork works well)
- a few vintage beads, crystals or broken diamante
- 1m (3ft) of 0.6mm wire
- a chain or clasp and some extender chain
- flat-nosed pliers and snips
- a small file

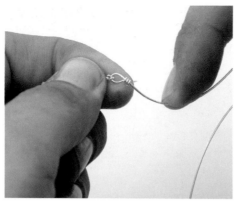

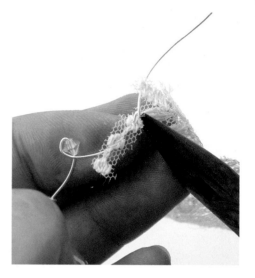

Top tip: This same design idea works really well as a cuff: just use a slightly larger piece of lace and shape your design around your wrist into an oval shape. Just add a shorter length of extender chain and lobster clasp with a jump ring and it's ready to wear as a pretty cuff.

1. After you've soaked the lace in watered-down PVA glue and allowed it to dry, snip around the part of the lace design you'd like to use. It's best to use a smaller piece than you might initially think you need, as you'll be building up the design with wirework.

2. Cut a length of the 0.6mm wire about 40cm (16in.) long. Make a loop at one end and attach it to the end of your chain (snipped in half) by wrapping the wire through the last link and back round on itself.

3. Smooth the wire with your thumb and forefinger to get a gentle curve.

   Then thread on one of your vintage beads and tightly wrap the wire round from one hole to the other.

4. Get your piece of lace ready and thread the wire through one corner of the design. Loop it round from front to back and then smooth the wire again into a curve in front of the lace.

5. Attach another bead in the same way as before then thread the wire back through the lace and out again (you're kind of 'sewing' big curvy stitches with the wire).

6. Carry on to the end of the lace design and do another small loop at the corner of lace.

7. Curve the wire again and attach another bead before making a small loop onto which you can attach the chain by wrapping the wire back on itself.

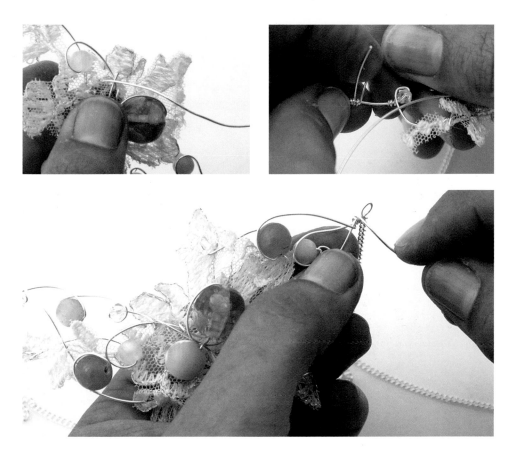

If you've managed to get your hands on a bit of vintage lace, it's really surprising how far it can go in making jewellery. You can easily stiffen it with watered-down PVA glue, then once it's dried you can pick out small chunks of the design with some small nail scissors. If you work in a few vintage beads and bits of diamanté, you'll only need a small piece of lace to make a really pretty, feminine necklace.

8. If you've got enough left, you can come back the other way with the wire, attaching beads and threading in and out of the lace as you go.

   It's a good idea to wrap the wire round the first row when you can (behind the lace, to hide the wire) to tether the design and stop it slipping.

9. It's nice to aim for a vaguely V shape, so if you need more wire, wrap another piece on top of the initial wrap near the first loop and continue the design from there.

10. Once you're happy with how it looks, wrap the leftover wire around the initial wrap and snip it off neatly.

   You might want to replace the clasp and attach some extender chain, with a bead charm on for the fastening, and then it is ready to wear.

There's something very ethereal and feminine about this cuff: the soft colours of the sea glass reflect the rock crystal beautifully, and if you can work in a bit of sparkle, tiny crystals can look like the sun glinting off the sea.

sea-glass crochet cuff

You will need:

- about 3m (10ft) of 0.4mm wire
- around 40–50 stones or beads (rock crystal, fluorite or jade chips work well)
- some sea glass (wire-wrapped, as on p.38)
- a hook or clasp
- flat-nosed pliers and snips
- a small file
- a crochet hook

1. Get a long piece of 0.4mm wire and make a loop in one end by wrapping it back on itself.

2. Put your crochet hook through this loop (from front to back)

   Wrap the wire once around the hook in a clockwise direction.

   Using the hook, pull the wire through the loop whilst pushing the loop off the hook. You should now have two loops joined.

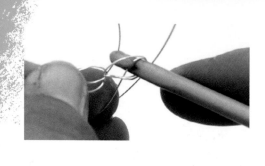

Top tip: If you crochet roughly the same amount as this cuff onto a torque (choker) base, you get a lovely, contemporary, focal necklace.

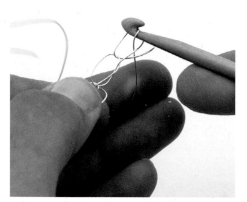

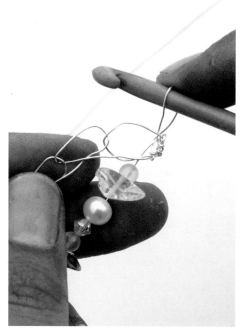

3. Continue with this movement so that your work starts to look like a chain. Try to keep it loose with biggish loops – it really doesn't matter if it's a bit messy and it will be a lot easier to work with if you can get the crochet hook in easily.

4. Make the chain just long enough to fit around your wrist – not too long, as you need to allow space for the clasp.

   Then pull the wire through and wrap it round a couple of times to stop the whole thing unravelling.

5. Now you're ready to attach some interesting bits and bobs. Cut a

1m (3ft) length of the wire and wrap it tightly four times around one end of your string chain.

6. Thread your beads and a couple of wrapped sea-glass pieces onto the other end of the wire. You'll probably need between 20 and 30 depending on how full you want it to look. Make a little loop at the end to stop them falling off.

7. Shuffle all these beads and finds to the end that's attached to the sea string. Put your hook through the first string-chain 'link' from front to back. Wrap the wire clockwise around the crochet hook and pull it through, pushing off the string

link. The wire should now have a loop attached to the string chain.

8. With this wire loop on the hook, put the hook through the next string link. Push the first bead or find right up to the hook then wrap the wire clockwise around the hook. Pull that wire through the first and then the second loop on the hook. You should have one loop left on the hook. If you have, well done!

9. Keep going with this technique all the way along the string chain. You can be fairly haphazard; just try to get some beads and glass to sit on the cuff in a random way – it's

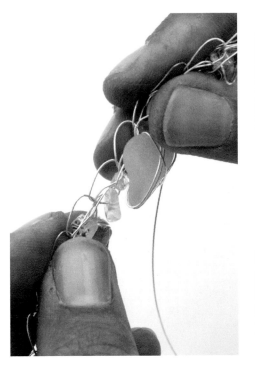

supposed to look messy and sea-weathered.

10. To make a deep cuff, you might want to join on another 1m (3ft) length of wire and go back along the cuff, attaching beads and sea glass in the same way as before; you can just keep going, adding extra rows till you get it as deep as you think looks good.

11. When you've had enough of crocheting, wrap the leftover wire through one of the final loops and then snip it off.

12. Shape and flatten the cuff with your fingers so all the beads sit as you want them to.

13. Then all you need to do is attach a largish hook onto one end by wrapping a 10cm (4in.) piece of 0.8mm wire round and through the cuff.

Shape the hook as shown, snip off the extra wire and gently file down any rough edges.

14. If you've sized it properly you should be able to hook it in several places so you can wear it looser like a bangle or tighter like a cuff, depending on your preference.

antique
wedding

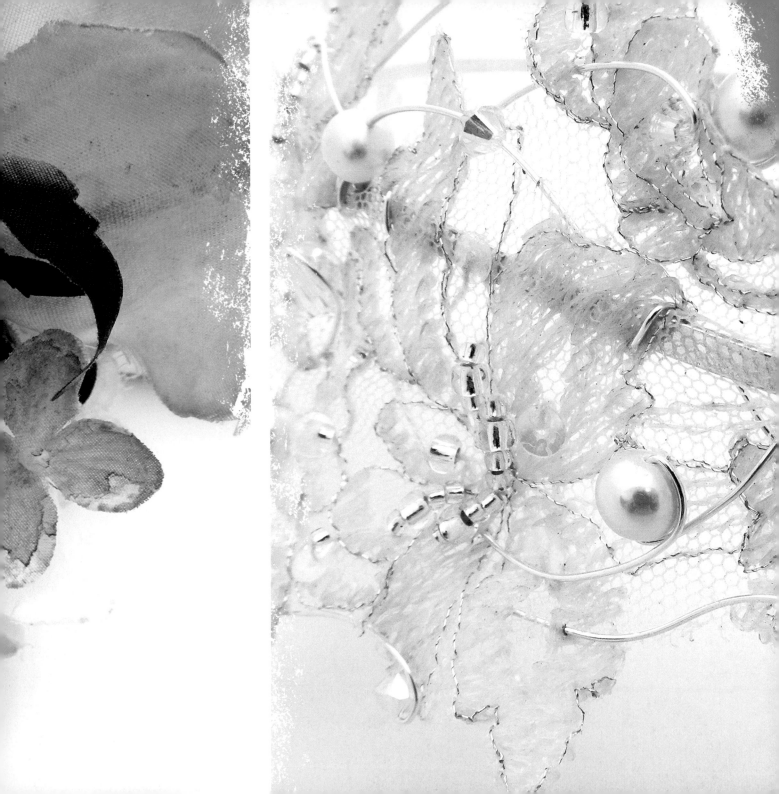

This is a lovely, dressy style that really showcases a vintage brooch find. The style of brooch you're using will probably give you a lot of direction for the design of the necklace, certainly in terms of the colour of beads you choose and the actual shape of the necklace. So just go with the vintage flow.

sparkly 1930s-style wirework necklace

You will need:

- an antique brooch of whatever colour, sparkliness or style you like (with a few open spaces in the design so you can attach it easily to the wirework)
- 2m (6ft) of 0.6 or 0.8mm wire (gauge depends on beads used and sturdiness required)
- A lobster clasp and extender chain or ribbon (50cm/20in.)
- A selection of beads (perhaps 20–30), sparkly vintage crystals, cut-up pieces of diamante and semi-precious stones look good
- pliers and snips
- a small metal file or nail file
- liquid superglue (optional)

Top tip: Make a little bead charm in a matching crystal to attach to the end of the extender chain. This will then hang down your back and nicely finish off your design's colour scheme.

1. Cut a length of wire about 60cm (24in.) long and make a loop at one end by wrapping the wire back around on itself about three times.

2. Choose your first bead and thread it onto the wire: stop it about 1cm (⅜in.) from the loop and then wrap the wire around the bead, from one hole to the other, to hold it in place where you want it to be.

3. Using your thumb and forefinger, smooth the wire into a curve (see picture above) and then add your next bead. Wrap the wire around it again from one hole to the other to hold it in place. You might want to

smooth the wire to curve in the other direction (i.e. upwards) so that the next bead sits differently. A bit of a random, organic look to the wirework makes it seem a bit more art nouveau!

4. After you've put on, say, three beads, start thinking about placing your brooch (or you might want to do a bit more wirework and place the brooch asymmetrically to one side). Before you attach it, remember to get your brooch ready by snipping the pin off the back; just snip through the pin first, close to the hinge and in a careful, controlled way so the pin doesn't become a flying missile.

5. Next gently snip the pin base in one direction then the other. The old base metals are normally quite soft so it may come away quite easily; if it's a bit tougher, just take your time and keep snipping round in different directions. Try not to pull the brooch backwards and forwards too much, as you could end up snapping it or losing stones out of the front.

6. When you've successfully removed the pin from the back, you'll need to file the sharp piece of metal left behind so it doesn't rub and irritate you. Once that's done you can attach the brooch to the beginning of your necklace

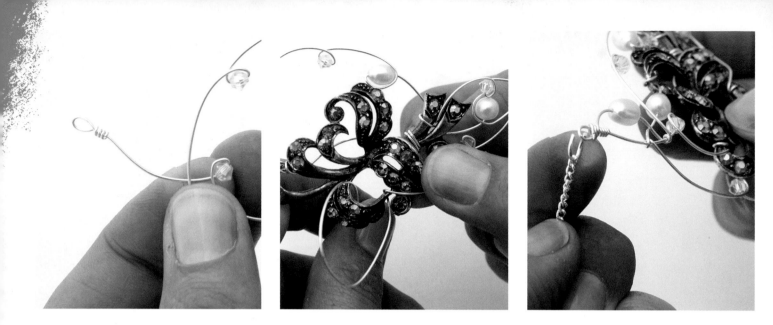

simply by finding a hole in the design, threading the wire through and wrapping it back on itself through the hole.

7. If you can aim to finish with the wire end at the back of the brooch it looks a bit neater.

8. Depending on how you want the brooch to sit on the necklace, take the wire to another part of the brooch (via the back) and wrap it through in the same way again. If you want the brooch to sit straight up, it'd be the other side; if you want it at an angle, you might skew it by taking the wire to the top or bottom.

9. Now the brooch is sturdily attached, you can carry on adding beads on the other side in a similar way as before, by

looping the wire from one bead hole to the other. You'll then be ready to put another loop on, and ready to attach the chain when you've finished.

10. You're aiming to make this front, focal wirework piece between 10 and 20cm (4 and 8in.) long depending on how bold you want it to be.

11. When you've made your second loop, start working back the other way provided you have about 30cm (12in.) or so of wire left, adding beads in the same way as before.

12. Wrap the wire once round the first row every 3–4cm (1¼–1½in.) to 'tether' it in place. You can wrap the brooch in again if necessary, or you can take the wire around the back of the

brooch. If you'd like some extra sparkle, you can thread beads onto the wire without wrapping them round; leave them loose and you can stick them with a little blob of superglue at the end.

13. When you get to the other end with your wire, wrap round the original loop two or three times to secure it, squeezing it with your pliers to make sure it's nice and tight. If you think your design needs some more shaping, add some more wire in the same place in the same way (as neatly as you can) and work your way back across and up or down your necklace.

14. When you're happy with the necklace shape, get a chain ready to attach to the wirework by snipping it at the

middle point. You then need to think about low you'd like the necklace to sit, taking into account that the wirework piece you've made is making the front length.

You often need to snip some of the length off the chain before you attach it to the wirework loops with jump rings.

15 It's also nice to change the clasp to incorporate an extender chain to keep your options open. This is a bit of a longer project, but it's worth it to create a real talking-point piece.

neat deco wire-wrapped bracelet

You will need:

- between five and seven vintage beads (round or oval) depending on your wrist size
- about 4m (13ft) of 0.6mm wire
- a clasp and some extender chain
- pliers and snips
- a small file

1. Using your snips, cut a length of wire around 50cm (20in.) long. Bend the wire about 6cm (2½in.) from one end and make a loop by wrapping the wire back round on itself. You should have a longish 'tail' so that you can continue wrapping around the wire eight times; I know it seems a bit odd, but it's quite important to count how many times you go round (so that the piece will be symmetrical later).

   Snip off the tail end.

2. Thread a bead onto the wire so that it presses right up to the wrapped wire section. Measure with your eye (or a ruler, if you'd like to be a bit more accurate) how far the first loop is from the bead and then make another loop of equal distance at the other end.

3. Wrap this around the same number of times as the first (eight) and you should reach the bead. Whatever you do, DON'T SNIP THE WIRE OFF! I often do, and it's very annoying: you need this long piece to do the deco wrapping with.

4. Take the wire around the bottom of the bead and wrap it over the top of the wrapped wire on the other side once so that the length of wire is at the top.

5. Take the wire snugly over the top of the bead.

Top tip: You could get some really big oval or round beads (3–4cm/1¼–1½in.) and make single, big, deco focal pieces for a long eclectic necklace or chain.

You might be lucky enough to get your hands on some oval vintage crystals to make into this deco-style bracelet; it also works well with pearls. I suppose it all depends on the colour or look of your wedding dress, and maybe what beads you're given for your 'something old'. In any case, the bracelet is a lovely, sophisticated style that you'll surely find the opportunity to wear again.

Wrap once over the top of the other wire wrapping so that the wire is ready to go around the bottom again.

6. Take the wire under the bottom of the bead, pressing it behind the initial wire wrap so that it doesn't stick out too much. Wrap the wire next to the one you did before, then take it back over the top again.

7. Continue in this way until you've covered all the initial wire wrapping and reached both loops. Just wrap round once and snip off the tail end.

8. Squeeze it with your pliers and file any rough ends.

9. You could make this into a pendant or an earring drop, but to make the bracelet you'll need probably five or six wrapped beads that you can join together with jump rings.

10. It might help to bend each deco piece slightly so that it fits nicely as a bracelet.

    Join the deco pieces together with jump rings.

11. Finally, attach a clasp to one of the end deco pieces, and a small length of extender chain to the other one, and it's done.

sophisticated asymmetric vintage headdress

You will need:
- one or more old brooches to fit in with the bridal theme (diamante, pearl or 1930s gold)
- a pre-made tiara base (see the list of websites on p. 104)
- 2m (6ft) of 0.6mm wire
- About 20 freshwater pearls
- About 10 different-sized crystals and possibly diamante (vintage ones are lovely, as not only do you get more for your money, but vintage diamante necklaces can be broken up and wired into your design)
- flat-nosed pliers and snips
- liquid superglue (optional)

1. Shape the tiara base by bending both ends outwards so the base has a horseshoe rather than a round shape – this makes it more comfortable to wear.

2. Start at about 10cm (4in.) up from the bottom of one side of the tiara base (you're aiming for the main part of the design to sit just above your ear). Cut a piece of 0.6mm wire about 20cm (8in.) long and wrap the middle part around the base at this point – wrap it around three or four times so it doesn't wobble.

3. Thread a pearl or crystal onto one of the wire ends and push it down so that it is near the base (about 1–2cm/¼–¾in. away). Take the wire all the way around the bead from one hole to the other so that the bead is snugly wrapped and firmly held.

4. Smooth the wire in a nice curve with your thumb and forefinger and then thread on another bead. Wrap this in the same way, from one hole to the other, though you might want to go round it in the opposite direction so that it sits on the other side of the wire branch.

5. Depending on the length of the wire, add two or three more beads: the last one looks nice if you wrap round it twice so that the bead is completely framed. Put some beads on the other length of wire in the same way.

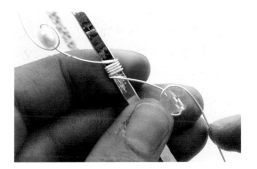

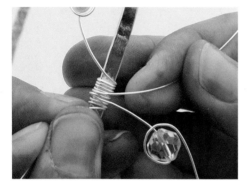

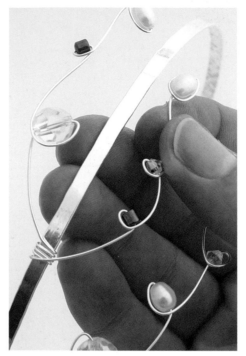

6. Thread beads and wrap them in the same way on the bottom piece of wire then attach perhaps two more lengths of wire coming from the same starting point, wrapped onto the base.

7. It's nice to vary the lengths a bit. Personally, I think it looks good with a few longer tendrils going backwards and perhaps a few shorter ones around the face.

8. Create a couple of shorter tendrils emerging from a point above this main part, and another couple lower down – it's entirely up to you. You should also consider how full you'd like it to look.

9. Try on the headdress as you go so as to gauge the proportions, as well as the possible hairstyles, that work best.

10. When you've got all the tendrils sorted you can think about attaching the wonderful vintage brooch that you've found. Get your brooch ready by removing the pin from the back. Using your snips, first simply snip through the pin, close to the hinge and in a careful, controlled way. Next gently snip the pin base in one direction then the other; the old base metals are normally quite soft and it may come away quite easily.

11. If it's a bit tougher, just take your time and keep snipping round in different directions. Try not to pull the brooch backwards and forwards too much, as you can end up snapping it or losing stones out of the front.

12. File down any rough edges of metal you might have left and then think about how you'd like the brooch to sit on your headdress: just hold one piece next to the other in different positions till you've found one that looks right.

13. Cut a piece of 0.6mm wire about 15cm (6in.) long, thread it through a hole on the brooch and then wrap it around the tiara base, wrapping both ends in different directions. Then thread it through another part of the brooch, at the other end, and wrap that around the base so that the brooch is held very firmly in place.

13. Snip off the tail end, squeeze the end with the pliers, and file any rough edges so that the inside feels smooth. Try it on and mess about with the tendrils until they look good with your hair, and there you are with the finished article: a beautiful, stylish headdress.

This is a lovely, stylish way of incorporating a family brooch or beads into your look, for your wedding day. You get the antique feel and personal connection from the brooch, but the headdress is updated with wild, growing beadwork that will suit most relaxed, fashionable hairstyles.

To balance a lacy, embellished dress, this headdress is great. Use some of the lace from your dress so that it matches exactly; or some vintage lace from your mum's or grandma's dress would be a lovely, personal touch.

antique lace headddress

You will need:
- a largish piece of lace
- PVA glue
- small scissors
- 2m (6ft) of 0.6mm and 0.4mm wire
- about 30 vintage pearls, diamante and crystals
- an antique brooch (or more than one, if you like)
- a tiara base
- pliers and snips
- a small file

Top tip: You could do a design with this lace style as the base and then include some naturally protruding tendrils (as in the asymmetric vintage headdress project) to build it up and out a bit.

1. Roughly cut out the piece of lace you want to use and soak it in some watered-down PVA glue. Let it dry out fully (this will probably be overnight). Once it's dry, cut around your lace design carefully with small (maybe nail) scissors. It's a good idea to pick a shape that can sit along the band but will also go backwards into the hair. This is quite a 1930s shape, and the sort of asymmetric headdress we're aiming for.

2. Bend the ends of the tiara out a bit to make more of a horseshoe shape, then snip a piece of wire about 30cm (12in.) long and wrap this around the base three times, about 5cm from one end.

3. Get a smooth curve to the wire by easing it with your thumb and forefinger, then thread on a chosen pearl or crystal. Hold it in place by snugly wrapping the wire around the bead from one hole to the other.

4. Next thread the wire through the lace, wrap it once around the base behind the lace, and bring the wire back to the front again to attach another bead.

5. Take the longer end and thread it though to the front of the lace at a middle point. Wrap it once around the base and continue to the far end of the lace piece, wrapping it round here about three times, going behind the lace as before.

6. Work your way around the lace in this way, adding beads till it's as full as you want it to be. But remember to leave a blank space where you'd like the antique brooch to be.

7. Get your brooch ready (as with the other vintage projects) by removing the pin from the back. First simply snip through the pin, close to the hinge and in a careful, controlled way. Then gently snip the pin base in one direction then the other. The old base metals are normally quite soft and it may come away quite easily; if it's a bit tougher, just take your time and keep snipping round in different directions. Try not to pull the brooch backwards and forwards too much, as you can end up snapping it or losing stones out of the front.

8. You can now add this to your lace base by just wrapping it on with a strand of 0.6mm wire about 15cm (6in.) long. Wrap it about three times at one end and the same at the opposite end to make sure it sits properly and doesn't wobble. And then it's finished. Well done.

golden 1930s leaves tiara

You will need:

- a vintage porcelain brooch
  (or similar colourful brooch)
- some florist's silk leaves sprayed gold
- a gold-plated tiara base
- 2m (6ft) of 0.6mm gold-plated wire
- pearls and coloured stones or crystals to match
- superglue
- pliers and snips
- a small file

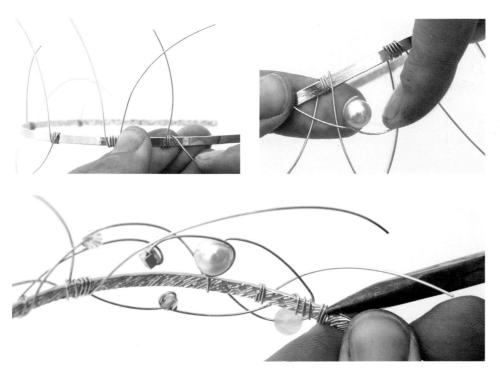

This is a lovely, extravagant vintage tiara that pays homage to all the lovely golden embellished china from the 1930s – a real eclectic vintage tea-party look, helped along by the antique porcelain rose brooch. I think it would look lovely with a slinky, warm ivory satin dress, or a crazy curly hairstyle for a Mad Hatter's tea-party look.

1. If you're thinking about using leaves in this design, get them ready by giving them a thorough coating of gold spray – I used 'antique gold' in this instance. That way they'll be dry when you're ready to use them.

2. Get your tiara base ready by bending each end outwards to form a horseshoe shape.

3. It's a good idea to get the sticking-up bits done first to give your design general structure. So cut a piece of wire about 15cm (6in.) long and wrap the middle point around the base three or four times at an off-centre position on the base (about 10cm/4in. from one end).

4. Trim these with your snips so that the left one is around 2cm (¾in.) longer than the right one. You can put the beads on later.

   Cut another, slightly shorter piece of the wire (about 10cm/4in. long) and wrap this around the base about 3cm (1¼in.) to the left of the initial pieces.

5. Ease one of these in the same direction as the longest one (as if growing towards the centre) and bring the other one below the band and gently bend it as if it's growing upwards.

6. Add another piece of wire in this same way on the other side (to the right) of the first pieces:

bend this new piece towards the initial one and trim it shorter. Then the other protruding piece can be bent away over the band.

7. You might want to add a few more little pieces further round to the left; then trim them so that they fit and complement each other nicely. Don't trim them too short, as you need to allow for losing a bit of height when you do the loop, to stop the stone falling off.

8. Cut a length of wire around 50cm (20in.) long and wrap it tightly around the band to the right, about 6cm (2½in.) from the end.

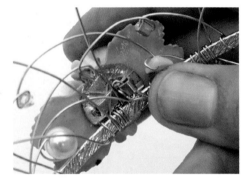

Top tip: If you'd rather wear an asymmetric, Alice-band headdress than a typical tiara shape, you can simply shift this design around the band. The long protruding pieces would be growing in parallel with the way the band sits in the hair, and you might want more pieces going over the head and down towards the ears.

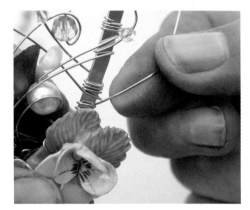

9. Get your vintage beads and diamante ready by breaking them up with your snips. Now you can start adding beads: thread on your chosen bead and wrap the wire from one hole to the other to tightly trap the bead.

   Smooth the wire into a nice curve with your thumb and forefinger before continuing to put on the next bead.

10. It's a good idea to tether this design to the base every 3cm or so. Once you get round to the other side, stop about 6cm (2½in.) from the end, wrap the wire round a few times then come back the other way,

taking the design higher and adding more beads.

11. When you get to the right side again, wrap the wire round a couple of times, snip off the tail end and then squeeze the wrapped wire with your flat-nosed pliers.

12. Take the pin off the back of the brooch as before (see p. 28), then cut a piece of wire around 10cm (4in.) long, ready to be attached.

13. Thread the wire through the loop that's left on the back of the brooch, then wrap both ends very tightly around the base, on top of the wrapping

for the highest-protruding pieces. Snip off the tail ends.

14. Think about which beads you'd like at the top of the protruding pieces: remember that they'll be quite high up, so don't choose beads that are too large or they'll end up looking like 'Deely Boppers'. Thread one onto each protrusion and then make a small loop at the top to stop the bead falling off.

15. Once you've got to this stage, you can have a good analytical look at your design and decide if it needs anything else. For one thing, it might be an idea to try it on and see how the proportions work. If you want

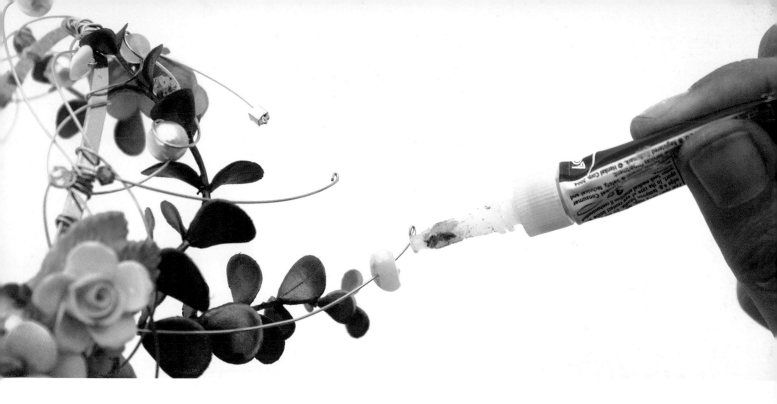

to make it a bit bolder and fill it out a bit you could do another row of the bead wirework; and you could also think about adding some gold-sprayed leaves.

16. The leaves can look lovely behind the porcelain brooch: if they're on florist wire, just wrap them around the base where you'd like them to sit; if not, just thread a short length of 0.6mm wire through the base of the leaf, make a firm loop, and wrap the wire around the base where you'd like it to be.

17 You might want to tether the leaves to the base with wire so they sit where you want them to.

18 Use your superglue to hold the top beads in place – it's easier if you hold the tiara upside down. Move the bead away from the loop for a minute, put a tiny drop of superglue next to the loop then quickly push the bead back up, over the glue, next to the loop. But be really careful: I know it may be stating the obvious, but superglue sticks really quickly and has no problem bonding thumbs and fingers. Your hand stuck to your glamorous tiara is not a good look.

19. And that's probably enough. You could go on adding more beads, diamante and even lace pieces if you're after a very extravagant, baroque sort of look. But if you're going for a more modern 30s style, then it's best to reign yourself in a bit, and aim for a simple overall shape.

selling
your work

pricing your work

Pricing what you've made is one of the most difficult things about selling jewellery – or anything else for that matter. You actually want to sell some pieces so you don't want it to be too expensive and put potential buyers off; yet if you price items too cheaply, people might think that they are low value and be put off wanting to wear them: it's quite a delicate, and not completely rational, balance. Retail companies employ people to spend their working lives pondering this problem. What's more, you could price your jewellery cheaply to be competitive, sell loads because people see it as a bargain, and then feel resentful and tired when you come to make them up again, because you know you're not getting what they are worth, meaning that you have to make a great number just to make a decent profit.

The straightforward way to approach this is to work out the minimum you could possibly, happily, charge for something. Then you have got this price as a non-negotiable bottom line, leaving you to be creative with how much you then charge depending on where you're selling your jewellery, the buyer, the general perception of its worth, the possible retailer commissions and basically how you feel on the day.

For example, decide what your minimum hourly rate is – I use £10 an hour. Then make a note of how much the materials for the piece have cost (you'll probably have to guess a bit, and make sure to round it up), and allow a bit for your marketing costs (the hire of a table at a craft fair, for example). So, for a bracelet that took half an hour to make, the price would be:

½ hour labour time	£5
materials	£2
marketing	£1
total	£8

Dead easy, really: the minimum I can charge for it is £8. I'd ideally want to make some profit on top of my labour time, so I'd probably hitch up the price to at least £10. This could be the wholesale price if I'm selling it to a shop or gallery, who will then probably double or triple that to sell it on to customers. But if I'm selling it direct to customers at a craft fair, for instance, it could easily be the retail price. If you're selling the same pieces both to shops and direct to the public, you might want to consider matching the shops' selling price so you don't annoy them and lose their business!

places to sell your jewellery

There're lots of different ways you can earn money from your jewellery, either enough to fund your making as a hobby or sufficient to earn a part- or even full-time living from a jewellery-making business. Most people tend to sell through a combination of markets:

To friends and family This is often the way people start out selling. It is hard to know if they are just doing you a favour sometimes, and it can be a bit awkward to know what you should charge. I'll often do them at a very low wholesale price or as a gift; or perhaps bartered for something like babysitting. It can be a good way of getting feedback on your designs, though; and if you're happy with the price you're charging and they don't grumble about it, why not?

At work This is quite a good captive market, especially if you work in a reasonable-sized office where people are a bit bored or there are loads of desperate men with no clue about present buying. It's up to you whether you ask your boss's permission or just whip out a board full of beautiful jewels when he or she is not looking. Some makers I know have just left jewellery nicely bagged up in a public area with an honesty box beside it. I suppose it depends on how honest your colleagues are.

Craft fairs Depending on where you live, you might see loads of craft fairs advertised in your area. These can be a very effective, cheap way of getting your jewellery seen by the public. But they can also be a waste of time. Taking into account how much you're planning on charging and how edgy or mainstream your jewellery is, the best thing is to be selective. It's hard to know in advance how good a fair will be, but, if you can, speak to people who went to the same event last year, look at how it's been advertised, and check out who else is going. You need to fit in with the feel of the fair, be able to comfortably afford the stall price and feel confident it will be publicised to the right market for you. It's no good taking bright, modern sea-plastic jewellery aimed at 20- to 30-year-olds to a small, country charity fair aimed at retirees. Having said that, don't underestimate the discerning taste and spending power of the older generation: you might just find you get a range going that is favoured by the older market group. Try to take along the most suitable range for each event. And sometimes you just have to bite the bullet and try out a few of these events to see what works best for you.

Through shops and galleries It's a bit nerve-wracking at first, approaching shops and galleries to see if they want to stock your jewellery. Which businesses are suitable and available depends of course on your location. In more touristy places you'll probably have lots of gift shops and small independent galleries that are ideal to ask; in cities there may be more independent clothes shops, specialist jewellery shops and even hairdressers which might consider displaying your products and taking a commission of the sale when pieces are bought I'd always recommend targeting independent shops or department stores rather than big chains (there's more chance of getting to see the owner/buyer, the person who can make a decision) and phoning or emailing in advance for an appointment – they probably won't appreciate you just dropping by. You simply have to ask if they'd be interested in seeing your new collection of jewellery, or if they'd like to stock your jewellery. Just say something straightforward and to the point, which feels natural to you. With any luck, you'll get an appointment. Then get yourself there on time, be open and flexible, and listen to what they're after.

You'll probably have to be prepared to offer items on a sale-or-return basis – they pay you as your items sell, not in advance – at least to begin with. As long as they seem trustworthy, and have a system in place to pay designers regularly, I think such an arrangement is fine, but you might need to be wary of businesses that don't stock other small designers, such as hairdressers and some bridal shops. And remember, most independent businesses really do want fresh products and are very receptive to trying out new designers, so just go and see them, show them what you've got, and be friendly.

Online with eBay/Etsy eBay can be a bit tricky for selling any jewellery you've made: people often use it to find a bargain and are normally very specific about their searches. However, it might work well if the pieces you're making use vintage pieces or specific stones that people might be searching for. And you'll probably have to be prepared to gamble a bit and start with a very low price. On the plus side, it's very cheap and reaches a massive audience, so it's definitely worth a try.

Etsy is like a craft version of eBay: it's US-based and, like eBay, you can just upload images of things you want to sell, paying a small fee (20¢) to list items and a percentage when things sell (3.5%). Like eBay, loads of people use it, and if you get good images of your work and the right title for your pieces (with words that people search for), you could do really well on it. There are English versions of Etsy too which might be more effective, with people keener to buy within the UK. Try www.folksy.com and www.misi.co.uk.

Jewellery parties If you have a wide circle of friends or acquaintances, jewellery parties can be a very effective way of selling. If you can create a relaxed atmosphere in a friend's home, it is likely people will happily buy from you. It's probably an idea to take pieces with a cross section of prices, starting from about £5, so that everyone can buy something, even if they're a bit skint. Most people feel that they should get at least one thing at these events, which is good news for you! You could pinch some ideas from other companies that work through parties, such as The Body Shop and Ann Summers: for example, they offer the hostess a gift, the value of which is based on how much her friends spend. Also, have a gift ready for anyone booking a follow-up party.

Wedding fairs A bit more specialised, but a good idea if you like making tiaras and special-occasion jewellery. It's not just the bride looking for jewellery to wear on the big day; there are bridesmaids and mothers to think about, too, so you can also take along jewellery with a bit of colour in it. However, don't expect to sell much at the fair: the brides are often planning at least months (sometimes years) in advance, so will probably want to meet up with you for a consultation at a later date. With this in mind, make sure you have loads of business cards, and a leaflet offering a discount on it sometimes works well too.

Trade shows These tend to be expensive (at least £1000 a time for a stand), so you'd probably need to have a good think about making that sort of financial commitment. Trade shows can be effective if you'd like to get wholesale customers elsewhere in the country (and maybe even overseas) without having to travel all over the place. Gift shows are good outlets for jewellery, as are bridal shows.

Have a go Hopefully, some of these ways of selling your work will appeal to you and seem manageable. I think the main things to consider are:

- what fits in with your life

- what exactly it is you're trying to sell (style and price)

- what you feel comfortable doing

- which events you can afford.

Have a go: you don't know till you try, and people tend to love jewellery and are happy to see it.

Whenever you do try a selling method, make sure you really listen properly to what people think of your work (even if it's not complimentary) so that you can tell what you're getting right and what wrong. It's very useful to get feedback if you want to sell your jewellery, so that you can make it both desirable and, dare I say it, commercial – this is not necessarily a dirty word!

conclusion

I hope you've enjoyed reading and using this book: I think the main things to remember are that this is just a starting point to give you ideas, and whatever you make is never wrong. It really doesn't matter if your version of a project looks completely different to mine. Just have a go and use whatever you can find or afford to make original jewellery; if you like what you make and can actually wear it somewhere on your body (without it causing you injury!) it really doesn't matter what anyone else thinks.

I often re-make things as well; make something, wear it for a while and then update it when fashions change and my outfits require different embellishment! That's the beauty of using free (or cheap) recycled materials: you're not too nervous to re-make them. And the benefit of having an open-minded, creative attitude towards jewellery-making, and gaining these new making skills means you can be as adventurous as you like with your own, individual jewellery designs. If you do get stuck or muddled about anything, or want to share a brilliant new creation, please just email me, I'd love to hear from you: info@sarahdrew.com. Happy foraging and have fun making!

useful websites for materials

www.beadaholique.com

www.beadexclusive.co.uk

www.beadmaster.com

www.beads.co.uk

www.beadsdirect.co.uk

www.beadsunlimited.co.uk

www.beadtime.com

www.beadykate.co.uk

www.constellationbeads.co.uk

www.cooksongold.co.uk

www.creativebeadcraft.co.uk

www.gjbeads.co.uk

www.internationalcraft.com

www.jillybeads.co.uk

www.justbeads.co.uk

www.kernowcraft.com

www.regalcrafts.com